God
Made Blue

Kelsey Heystek

Fulton Books, Inc.
Meadville, PA

Published by Fulton Books 2021

ISBN 978-1-63710-039-4 (paperback)
ISBN 978-1-63710-041-7 (hardcover)
ISBN 978-1-63710-040-0 (digital)

Printed in the United States of America

Did you know God made the colors?
He really did. It's true!

He made red, green, orange, and
yellow...and He even made blue!

God Made Red

God made the color red
He made it plain to see
Bright as the apples
That hang on a tree.

He made round red tomatoes
Shiny strawberries too
God used the color red
On all sorts of food!

How about the leaves on the trees
That turn red in the fall?
Red flowers-like roses!
God made them all.

What other red things
Did our Creator make?
Birds with red feathers
And red scales on snakes.

Tiny red ladybugs
Crawling on the ground
Sparkly red rubies
So precious to be found!

There is one more place
We see the color red
A crown of thorns
Placed on Jesus's head

Red holes in His hands
Red holes in His feet
Red stripes to His back
Taken for you and for me.

So when you think of red
Think of what Jesus did for us
Think of amazing grace
And of God's unending love.

God Made Orange

God made the color orange
What a fun color to see!
When autumn returns
There are orange pumpkins and leaves!

Oranges themselves
Make a sweet juicy snack
And have you ever seen soft orange
Fur on a cat?

God takes His paintbrush
And colors the sky
With beautiful streaks of orange
As the sun rises high.

8

Carrots are orange
And some flowers are too!
Many fish in the deep
Have a pretty orange hue.

Bright are the orange feathers
On the birds as they sing
God even made butterflies
With orange on their wings.

God made fire orange
As it flickers so bright
It burns orange like the sky
When the sun goes down for the night.

Orange frogs and monkeys
Tigers with orange stripes!
Orange foxes and polar bears...
Oh no, wait, those are white!

So as you can tell
Orange is easy to spot
God has used it in creation
Quite a lot!

God Made Yellow

God made the color yellow
You've seen it around
Maybe in the dandelions
Sprouting from the ground.

13

Can you think of all the yellow
Foods that God made?
Bananas, corn, and pineapples...
Lemons that make sweet lemonade.

Sunflowers and daffodils
Grow pretty and bright
They stretch toward the sun
With its bright yellow light.

14

Buzzing bumblebees
With stripes yellow and black
God put stripes on snakes too,
To say "Hey, just stay back!"

Fuzzy yellow chicks and canaries
Flying through the sky
And God made chickens to lay eggs
With yellow yolks inside!

Some leaves on the trees
Turn yellow in the fall
God made so much yellow
And we love it all!

16

God Made Green

God made the color green
Just take a look around
So many different shades
Of green to be found!

17

Trees and plants of every kind
Have velvety green leaves
Frogs and turtles, chameleons too
God made them all in green.

Think of all the foods you eat
That God made the color green
Kiwis, apples, limes, and grapes
Broccoli, lettuce, and peas!

So many little bugs are green
Have you seen any crawling along?
And don't forget the pine trees
That stay green all winter long!

Have you ever seen a peacock?
Their feathers shimmer green and blue
Parrots and little hummingbirds
Have green feathers on them too!

19

To see more green that God has made
There is one more place to look
He tells us all about it
He wrote it in His Book!

As a Shepherd, He leads His sheep
Beside the quiet streams
And there He helps us find our rest
In pastures soft and green.

God Made Blue

God made the color blue
It's very easy to find
Look outside on a sunny day
And see the bright blue sky!

God's ocean is so deep and wide
With rolling waves of blue
If you swam under its surface
You'd find some blue fish too!

Can you think of something blue
That can fly up in the sky?
That's right! God made bluebirds,
And blue jays, and big blue butterflies

Have you ever seen a peacock?
Their feathers are blue and green
God made some frogs in the bluest blue
That you've ever seen!

Flowers with blue petals
Blue lobsters in the sea
God even made some blueberries
That make a tasty treat!

All these things are pretty neat,
These things that God made blue
But none of them are quite as great
As the way that God made you!

God wanted to show us His beauty
with the colors that He made.
So when we see them everywhere, we
remember our God is great!

About the Author

 Kelsey Heystek was born and raised in Northwest Iowa and developed a love for writing when she was ten years old. She continued to polish her writing abilities throughout her school years, which culminated in a BSN degree in the spring of 2016. In the fall of 2016, she was married and now lives in Everson, Washington, with her husband, Darren. She enjoys being a busy stay-at-home mother to two-year-old Camden and six-month-old Aria. This book is dedicated to her children and their colorful personalities. She and Darren are so thankful to have the gift of raising their kids to know and love their Heavenly Father, who created all things for the glory of His Holy Name.

For more from the author, visit https://kelseykooima.wixsite.com/fullnessofjoy.